596
SC O
KSB
cop. 21

P9-CCM-163

8.95

j596
SC

Scott, Jack Denton

City of birds and
beasts

DATE			

COP. 21

WITHDRAWN

Knox-Sullivan
Bookmobile

© THE BAKER & TAYLOR CO.

CITY OF
BIRDS AND BEASTS

Knox-Sullivan
Bookmobile

Rainey Memorial Gates

CITY OF BIRDS AND BEASTS

Behind the Scenes at the Bronx Zoo

JACK DENTON SCOTT

With photographs by Ozzie Sweet

Knox-Sullivan
Bookmobile

G. P. PUTNAM'S SONS   NEW YORK

596
Sco
KSB
Cop. 2

ACKNOWLEDGMENTS

My thanks and appreciation to everyone at the Bronx Zoo for help that went far beyond the call of duty: the indefatigable general director; the curators, supervisors, superintendents, and their assistants; the most able keepers; the zoo police; the gatekeeper; the effective secretaries in the administration building; the versatile veterinarian. The Bronx Zoo is the happy sort of place where even the animals, the birds, and the boa constrictors cooperate.

J.D.S.

Copyright © 1978 by Jack Denton Scott
All rights reserved. Published simultaneously in Canada by
Longman Canada Limited, Toronto.
Printed in the United States of America
Design by Kathleen F. Westray

Library of Congress Cataloging in Publication Data
Scott, Jack Denton.
City of birds and beasts.
Summary: Describes the organization and daily operation of the 252-acre Bronx Zoo.
1. New York (City). Zoological Park—Juvenile literature.
{1.—New York (City). Zoological Park. 2. Zoological gardens}
I. Sweet, Ozzie. II. Title.
QL76.5.U62N4828   596'.007'40147275   77-13888   ISBN 0-399-20633-7

This is for BONNIE, *who had the idea—*
and for DAVID, *who made it work.*

A black-necked screamer greets the day.

THIS day will dawn fair on what was Jonas Bronck's farm, twelve miles from the center of Manhattan. But despite a brilliant summer sun, four storms will thunder, and lightning will flash over parts of these 252 acres of land that contain six deserts, four swamps, four rain forests, a fourteen-foot waterfall, one beach, a seacliff, seven jungles, two caves, an African savannah, a South American pampa, an Arctic tarn, and a prairie.

All, including the thunderstorms, are man-made. They are mainly for the benefit of New York State's most exotic residents: 1,037 mammals, 1,748 birds, 521 reptiles, and 75 amphibians. The old Dutch farmer's land, bisected by the Bronx River and two of its tributaries, is the home of the world-famous Bronx Zoo.

Few of the 38,000 who will visit today will realize the complexity of running this city of birds and beasts for their pleasure. Two hundred and seventy full-time employees (some of them beginning as teenagers, tending ponies and camels, then graduating to animal keepers) work, mostly behind the scenes, to keep this great zoo's complicated machinery functioning as smoothly and unobtrusively as that of a simple city park. (In summer their numbers swell to 650.)

Control is maintained by dividing the numerically cumbersome operation into three departments: Birds, Mammals, and Reptiles. At the top is the general director, who has an assistant; each of the three divisions is headed by a curator, also with assistants; under them are senior and assistant superintendents; and under them, the people who have the most direct contact with the animals, birds, and reptiles—the senior keepers and the keepers. The Mammal Department also has two supervisors who work directly under the curator.

This simple structure is one reason for the zoo's success at a time when many zoos nationwide are under attack by conservationists and animal lovers for being poorly run. Organization is tight and effective, with all employees personally accountable for their responsibilities. No bureaucratic buck-passing is tolerated.

Another reason for success is the general director, William Gaylord Conway, an imaginative zoologist and ornithologist with an international reputation that brings delegations from everywhere to study the Bronx Zoo. Actually, the zoo is the Zoological Park of the New York Zoological Society, which Conway also directs and which includes the New York Aquarium. The Society was established in 1895, dedicated to the study, conservation, and protection of wild animals worldwide. With seventy projects in more than forty countries, the Society has not only studied bird, mammal, and reptile life but has sent its people around the world to enlist help for endangered animals.

The Bronx Zoo is the venerable Society's showcase where Conway puts his tomorrow philosophies into effect today,

A Masai ostrich

among them his belief, first among many zoologists, that it is impractical to maintain large numbers of many species. Several years ago the zoo had 2,600 animals of 1,100 species. Conway flatly asserted that no zoo can possibly manage 1,000 different species of animals soundly or begin to exhibit them meaningfully. Today his zoo has about 3,077 animals, but of only 711 species. Thus, the Bronx Zoo is a producer, not a consumer, of wild animals. Each year the zoo rears more animals and birds than it acquires from any other source. It supplies other zoos with rare and difficult-to-obtain species.

Conway modestly cuts his view of zoo operation to the philosophical bone. He feels that his zoo is an outpost of a national park in a city; that by exhibiting representatives of such species as the rhinoceros, crocodile, and antelope, the zoo is also asking the city dweller to protect them. "We individualize animals," Conway says. He also is successfully turning attention away from a zoo as a prison, concentrating on the ways of animals in nature, and he looks forward to the day when he won't have a cage on the premises.

The hour before the sun rises and most of the zoo stirs is the demanding preparation time for the most important function at the Bronx Zoo: feeding the animals and birds, which is done at an annual cost of $250,000. Amazingly, this readying of food is performed mostly by one man, who ticks off feeding facts as some of us do baseball scores.

A young Kodiac bear eats twenty-five pounds of dog chow a day, plus five pounds of apples, two pounds of chicken parts, two and a half pounds of fish, and a generous lacing of fresh oats and barley sprouts. An elephant munches $4,000 worth of fodder yearly, and an active hummingbird must daily eat four times its own weight of an exotic food concocted by the zoo.

The visitors themselves bring large appetites to the zoo. In less than five months visitors consume 300,000 hot dogs, 100,000 hamburgers, 85,000 ice-cream specialties, plus countless lunches ranging from tuna and ham salads, cold-cut platters, knockwurst and sauerkraut, to roast beef. One hundred and fifty cafeteria and restaurant workers are prepared to feed two and a half million zoogoers who come yearly to see the wild animals, birds, and reptiles that many of them never forget.

4:45 A.M.

THE moon has faded. Night hangs over the zoo black as swamp water. From Wolf Woods the howls of the four tundra wolves, triggered by a fire engine's siren screaming through dark Bronx streets a few minutes ago, rise and carry on the night wind, a wild, strangely disturbing sound in this hour before dawn. The haunting tremolo of the two females

Tundra wolves at dawn

lasts longer than that of the males. Then it is abruptly silent. One of the frustrations of the curator of mammals is that he seldom succeeds in tempting the wolves to howl in response to the tapes of other wild wolves' chorusing. But sirens never fail.

Free-roaming peacocks, always awake before sunrise, mew like tomcats from atop their tree roosts. On Lion Island a lion roars, a sound like the beating of a bass drum. A sea lion's bark sounds far away, the voice of a weary hound.

—— 4:50 *A.M.* ——

GEORGE FIELDING, in charge of the Animal Commissary, the first man to move in this darkest time of day, unlocks the door, switches on the lights, and vaguely hears the sounds. The lights suddenly flashing on in the commissary isolate it in the compound and in the entire zoo like a lonely island looming out of a dark sea. The bearded, brown-haired, thirty-eight-year-old Fielding has been unlocking the door and hearing the zoo sounds at this hour for twelve years. He would be startled if he didn't hear them. They are part of the normal routine.

The Animal Commissary used to be located on "Slaughterhouse Hill," where fresh meat was prepared for the carnivorous animals. But now, Fielding, under the direction of the zoo veterinarian, Dr. Emil Dolensek, helps the keepers prepare a more varied and balanced diet.

Like the majority of zoo employees, Fielding, a veteran of twenty years' service, has worked in other departments and was a mammal keeper before being transferred to the commissary. Yesterday he drove 120 miles northeast of New York City, to Taconic Farms, in Germanville, New York, where laboratory animals are raised. The zoo has two freezers there, holding rats and mice it buys for the reptiles; these rodents are culls too large or too small for the laboratories. Fielding buys 40 bags (150 pounds to the bag) of frozen rats every month and 15 bags of mice. Sometimes he picks up 100 live rats or 1,000 live mice at a bargain, 40 cents a rat, 18 cents a mouse. The going price usually is 75 cents for rats, 27 for mice.

5:15 A.M.

TONY AUILES, who will deliver the food to each installation, clatters up to the commissary in a panel truck and parks it beside the loading platform.

Fielding, working with speed born of long routine, has the first load on the platform: food for the Bear Den, World of Birds, World of Darkness, Lion House, Penguin House, and Elephant House. All portions are for two days. Fielding separates and stacks a total of 200 pounds of mackerel; 24 pounds of smelts; 208 pounds of special feline diet, formed into blocks, mostly raw horsemeat with vitamins and minerals added; 60 pounds of chicken parts; 100 pounds of fresh-ground horsemeat; 8 pounds of horse hearts; 210 fresh eggs; 17½ pounds of blueberries; 118 pounds of apples; 76 pounds of carrots; 21 pounds of yams; 86 pounds of bananas; 2 pounds of grapes; 21 pounds of bread; 46 pounds of oranges.

It adds up to an enormous amount of lifting and parceling. Perspiration stands on Fielding's forehead like drops of rain.

But he helps Tony load the truck, for timing is important.

Delayed feeding means restless animals. Tony reverses, is about to back out, when Fielding calls, "Hey, wait a minute! I forgot the polar bears' lollypop!" He hurries to the freezer and gets a bucket containing three mackerels frozen in ice. They will slide out in a solid block, a plaything and a snack for the white bears.

He doesn't forget the special diet for the toothless ant-eaters, which eat with their tongues the well-balanced mixture of eggs, evaporated milk, three pounds of chopped horsemeat, bonemeal, and one box of breakfast cereal. And he remembers that the chunks of meat for the birds of prey must be more bone than meat, so that the birds' beaks wear down normally, as they would in the wild.

Tony will stop by the trailerlike installations near the Reptile House and pick up some of 1,000 pounds of wheat, oats, and barley sprouts that are raised hydroponically every week. This is done in a chemical soup in thirty-four trays, a process the zoo is proud of and will expand. Most of the tender sprouts will be fed to the mammals, but the birds will get their share, too.

5:30 A.M.

FIELDING takes thirty seconds to walk onto the platform and watch the sun edge up above the horizon. It will be a nice day.

Fielding will have all of the 290 food items delivered to the 14 other installations by 7:30 A.M., then wash down the refrigerator floor, the entire commissary floor, and the platform. Dr. Dolensek, knowing that the proper food delivered promptly pushes the entire zoo into normal motion, thinks Fielding does the work of three men.

6 A.M.

FROM where he sits, high in a tree, the curly-haired young man convinces himself that this new sun filtering through the branches is as clear as spring water. For him it is the best hour of the day. He appreciates the cock pheasant's coarse, defiant crowing from the nearby wildfowl aviary and waits for the bell-like morning roar of Yago, the male Siberian tiger that paces in an outside cage at the Lion House. Then he raises binoculars and watches the action, beneath him, in the South American area, of two cavies that resemble large, small-eared rabbits. He has previously tagged them and watched them bear twin offspring.

This is Mark MacNamara, who has a doctorate in mammalogy and is assistant curator of mammals, here on his own time before the zoo day begins, studying *maras*, or South American cavies. He will watch them every day for a month, then every other day, then twice a week for five months. He

The cavies with their twin offspring

is concerned because the young have not been surviving. He wants to know why. Mark will study them in depth here, then go to South America and observe them in their natural habitat.

Suddenly, he hears an uproar from the rhea area; the big, ostrichlike birds run and flap their wings. Mark sits stunned, unbelieving.

A man in the enclosure is stripping tail feathers from a rhea that screams in terror. Mark instantly summons zoo security on the walkie-talkie many zoo employees wear on their belt.

When he sees Joe Spadafino, of the zoo police, quickly arrive on his cycle, Mark slides down the tree. Together they approach the man.

Seeing them advancing, the man turns to flee, but stops, knowing it is useless. Hands full of feathers, he grins sheepishly.

═══════ *6:15 A.M.* ═══════

DISGUSTED, Mark MacNamara walks to the Lion House, which holds no lions but does have other large cats. In a morning routine that has become a ritual that buoys his spirits, he stops at an outside cage, says softly, "Shanda, Shanda." From a cavelike area at the rear of the cage, out bounds a magnificent snow leopard. Mark rubs her nose with a forefinger as she presses against the bars, and she purrs. This animal, rare now, even in nature, was five weeks old when its mother died. Most of the curators and some of the assistant curators live at the zoo. Mark and his supervisor, Curator of Mammals James Doherty, have an animal nursery behind their apartments. They took turns caring for the leopard cub for three months, feeding it six times a day for two weeks, and then, finally, at 6 A.M., noon, 6 P.M., and mid-

The Lion House, famous in zoo architecture, with sculpture and bas-relief

night. Although the cub was healthy, Mark was worried, as he is about all hand-reared animals that do not have contact with others of their own age. But this turned out well. They acquired Khan, a male from the Lincoln Park Zoo, only two days younger than Shanda. Khan is back there now, in the recessed area of the cage, still asleep.

6:20 A.M.

A DISTURBING situation has brought John Behler, curator of reptiles, in early. Behler, who gets more trying, beyond-duty requests than any other curator, will be tried several times this day. His two top assistants, Superintendent Pete Brazaitis and Senior Keeper Bob Brandner, are here in the Reptile House with him.

Ridgewood, New Jersey, has rushed in five live rattlesnakes. The community needs a quick answer to two questions that have the entire town atremble. "Are these wild snakes that somehow have invaded our area? Or are they snakes that have been released?"

Thirty timber rattlers were captured in Ridgewood's shopping and parking areas, all found within a 600-yard area. Townspeople claim to have seen at least three times that many.

One by one, Behler, Brazaitis, and Brandner carefully pin down and examine the three-foot snakes. If untreated, a bite from this type of rattlesnake can kill within forty-five minutes.

Behler's report:

1. All snakes are extremely emaciated, probably not fed in a month, have no fat reserve. At this time they should have maximum fat deposits.
2. All have old wounds, healed, but indicative of rough handling during captivity.
3. They have been improperly boxed, have shed skins, but pieces of "sheds" are still on them. Snakes' nostrils are raw from constantly probing for places in the box from which they could escape.
4. One snake is dying of amebiasis, a disease peculiar to captive snakes under stress, cramped quarters, improper food.

Behler's assessment: These are captive snakes recently and deliberately released.

——— *6:45 A.M.* ———

AT two desks in a large room in the Lion House sit Richard Bergmann and Fred Sterling, the two Mammal Department supervisors, who for all practical purposes run the department, the curator mainly handling major problems and decisions.

As they sit drinking lukewarm coffee, men start filing in—
the twelve senior keepers of the Mammal Department. They
are checking in before going about their daily duties. The
other departments do not have this routine, and that is all it
actually is. The keepers know where they are going, but au-

An appealing leading lady of the elephants

tomatically the supervisors say, "Cosmo, World of Darkness; Howie, Ape House; Lawston, Elephant House."

This, however, is an effective routine, for it gives keepers and supervisors an opportunity to discuss problems before the zoo day starts. Bergmann says to Lawston, "How is Cutie?" She is the leading lady of the elephants, a forty-year-old Indian elephant that has been at the zoo for thirty-five years and is loved by both visitors and keepers.

Lawston, poking fun at Sterling, who has been a supervisor for only a few weeks, sobers immediately. "Not good," he says. "She isn't eating, can't seem to sleep, is getting touchy. We've got problems, I'm afraid, Dick."

"Want me to report it to Jim?" Jim is James Doherty, curator of mammals.

Lawston shakes his head. "I'll put it in my report." All senior keepers make out a daily report, detailing the state of their department each day. This is carefully studied by the curator, and if action is needed, it is taken immediately.

As the keepers leave, Bergmann looks thoughtfully at Sterling. The young man has been promoted to supervisor over all the other keepers—some of them older, more experienced men—but Bergmann has detected no resentment. He thinks he knows the reason. Not only is Sterling very able; he is a quick thinker in an emergency and has the respect of everyone in the Mammal Department. Bergmann can still hear the words of one keeper of the Monkey House who told about the morning Sterling could have been seriously injured. That keeper was fired shortly afterward for not assisting Sterling. Secretly, Bergmann sympathized somewhat with the man. Facing a fierce seventy-five-pound hamadryas baboon, an animal of great strength, with canines larger that a dog's, out of its cage, takes know-how and courage. This keeper didn't have enough of either, so there was no place for him at the zoo.

"We arrived and saw the baboon in the service area," the keeper reported. "Fred saw the lock dangling. 'No one's fault,' he said. 'Defective lock. He sprung it. No danger. He's trapped in the service area.'

" 'How do we get him back in his cage?' I said.

"That baboon is humping and growling, long teeth showing, acting like he owns the place and wants a fight. He's a sly, mean one.

"Fred is thinking. Finally he says, 'He's in control of the service area. Too much space. If we can get in there with him, open that other door, and get him into that smaller back room, we can handle it.'

"I told Fred I better stay where I am, in case I am needed to get more help fast. Fred didn't say anything, but he moved.

"He edged quietly into the service room. But the baboon heard him and whirled around, screaming. Fred rushed right by him and opened the other door, leading into the small room where he wants to get the baboon.

These ring-tailed lemurs live in the Monkey House.

"The baboon is fast. He grabs Fred. I think he's going to tear him apart. I've seen that baboon smash a metal pail like a paper cup. But Fred stays cool. He stands very still, bends way over, his head touching the floor, in the submissive attitude of the female. But he's no female baboon. I wonder what's going to happen.

"The baboon keeps screaming. He tears Fred's shirt into shreds. I think he's going to keep tearing until Fred's a bloody mess. But he stops. Still screaming, he moves through the door Fred opened.

"Fred slams the door. The baboon rages against it, still screaming at him.

"Fred walks out, puts on another shirt, and calls the Curator."

6:55 A.M.

THE Lila Acheson Wallace World of Birds has no counterpart. In the early morning light its rounded, sweeping contours gleam like the Taj Mahal, and its sophisticated, imaginative structure has set the pace of zoo exhibition for years to come. This area contains a tropical rain forest, a desert, an Australian outback, and much more; here visitors view natural, wild bird life in the treetops; here is such a marvel of created environment that there is no barrier between public and birds. The birds are completely free, their own areas so perfect for all of their needs that they have no reason to try to fly away.

Up on the roof, a keeper is collecting live insects trapped at night through an ingenious system: Attracted by ultraviolet lights, insects are sucked into bags by constantly revolving fans. They will be fed to the insectivorous species, but the World of Birds has also trained the birds to eat other food prepared by its specialist, Senior Keeper Vincent Pepe.

6:58 A.M.

BELOW, in the kitchen, Pepe and his assistant, Stephen Diven, have cooked 210 eggs and 50 pounds of ground horsemeat and mixed them into the much-used "soft food," ground carrots, ground corn, raisins, rice, vitamin E and nutrients, ground raw meat, bananas, grapes, apples, and blueberries. The World of Birds' 700 residents will be fed now, and again at 1:30 P.M.

Meanwhile, Pepe mixes the special "nectar" upon which the hummingbirds thrive, blending a mixture of condensed milk; super-Hydramin, a vitamin-protein-mineral powder; Mellin's food, strong with malt, milk modifier, iron and thiamine; honey, and beef extract. This nectar is placed in gravity-fed bottles among flowers.

A hooded vulture and an emu

7 A.M.

NOT far from the kitchen, Chief Ornithologist Joseph Bell stands watching Senior Superintendent Andy Winnegar. The silvery-haired Bell is the zoo exception, a keeper who started here in 1942, made senior keeper in 1957, and in 1972 became curator of birds. Rarely do keepers become

curators. Today, the highly respected Bell has advanced to overseer of the Department of Ornithology. His former assistant, Donald Bruning, is now curator of birds.

Brawny Andy Winnegar, using forceps to feed a baby bird, has a hobby of teaching swimming, weightlifting, and scuba diving at a YMCA. Watching, Bell recalls a day not many months ago when a keeper came running to Winnegar in the afternoon as he was feeding his birds, shouting that two boys had fallen through the ice on the zoo's Lake Agassiz and were in danger of drowning. Rushing to the lake, discarding his clothing as he ran, Andy dived into the icy water, swam to the ice ledge, where the screaming boys were still hanging on, and rescued them. He was given a citation by the commissioner of police at a public ceremony.

Right now, Andy, who has the most knowledgeable, gentle hands of any keeper, is feeding a Malayan banded pitta, so rare in captivity that Andy himself raised the first one. Pitta do lay eggs, but chicks that hatch live only one day. This pitta, weighing six grams, mouth agape, is being carefully fed pieces of "pinky," naked baby rat, alternated with small, moistened dog-food pellets. It will be fed every hour for the next two days, then every two hours for two weeks. Weight is charted daily, using a special scale that registers as little as a quarter of a gram.

As he finishes feeding the bird, Andy looks into the incubators, which so far this year have held more than 2,000 fertile eggs. Depending upon species, eggs take twelve to forty-eight hours to hatch. After thirty-six hours, if the un-hatched birds do not begin piping with their egg tooth, Andy, his assistant, or one of the other seventeen keepers assists.

Andy has checked his daily log, knows that one egg isn't piping naturally. Carefully, he breaks off a tiny piece of its shell, sprays the egg lightly with water, to stimulate the bird into breaking its way out. Skill is required; too much of the eggshell should not be broken, as the bird must make most of the struggle itself in order to absorb the yolk sac which is necessary for it to sustain life. While making the effort to get out of the shell, the bird pulls the yolk into its body.

——— *7:10 A.M.* ———

MAKING conversation, Bell asks Andy how many birds were hatched last year. The superintendent has the figures in his head: "Six hundred and fifty hatched, four hundred fifty-six raised, half by hand." Andy pauses dramatically. "You're aware, aren't you, that at one point we hand-reared sixteen hundred birds."

Bell laughs and says he's impressed. He knows that wild birds raise only ten percent of their hatched young. Here at the World of Birds, amazingly, Andy Winnegar and his staff raise more than fifty percent.

As Andy, skillful as a mother bird, feeds a baby Burmese red-humped woodpecker, perhaps the only young specimen of its kind ever to be raised in captivity, Bell thinks of the unusual chores zoo workers perform and the demands made upon them. He recalls an incident that remains vivid in his memory.

One stormy night twenty hummingbirds of five exotic species had arrived at Kennedy Airport from Ecuador. Not wanting to send any of his staff out at midnight in such weather, Bell went to get them. Knowing there are always emergencies, he brought along a carrying cage, rope, twine, water, first-aid kit, pliers, hammer, nails, rubber tape, and a supply of special hummingbird nectar.

When he arrived at Kennedy, a freight clerk showed him the birds and told him they were all dead. Carefully, Bell examined each tiny bird, felt some warmth and faint heartbeats. Also examining the long wooden box in which they had been shipped, he quickly saw that the shipper had economized, stretching cord across the width of the box instead of a wooden perch. If a heavier bird jumped onto the cord perch, the smaller birds were bounced off. This, plus not getting the food that their enormously high metabolism demanded, had so exhausted the hummingbirds that they had collapsed.

Remembering a technique taught him by an old keeper, Bell, with the airport attendants staring in amazement, stuck the long bill of each bird into his mouth. When he felt the tiny tongue flicking out to taste the sugar in his saliva, he quickly dipped each beak into the special nectar he had brought. All birds were revived.

Arriving back at the zoo at 4 A.M., Bell had to repeat the procedure. He didn't get to bed at all that night, but the hummingbirds lived. In fact, one of the birds gave the zoo a world record for hummingbird longevity, living ten years, seven months, and seven days.

7:30 A.M.

SENIOR Keeper Howard Diven opens the door of the Ape House. He has been below in the service area for some time, preparing food. Now there is an ominous quiet. His Lowland gorillas are like children in the morning, greeting him vociferously with grunts, hurrying out to meet him. He makes a rapid check of their cages; the two big males, Bendera and Chuma, are all right. Chuma is not acting the clown this morning, holding a hand to his ear as if listening, as he always does when awaiting his morning meal. The females, Mwasi, Tunuka, and the neurotic Sukari, are also all right, but they seem somewhat subdued. Even the four-year-olds, Mopi and Hodari, are strangely quiet.

Howie is surprised that Keeper Peta Rader, the 24-year-

Chuma is serious.

old English girl, isn't here. She was surrogate mother to these two young apes, which had been rejected by their mothers. She had sat in the cage with them six hours a day for two years, providing the security and comfort that their natural mothers had not. Shortly after that, the two little apes had begun their famous Picasso-like finger painting, the unique

591
sco
KSB
COP. 2.1

art in great demand by visitors. Then, abruptly, last year, to the chagrin of zoo and visitors, the apes lost interest.

Approaching the last cage, Howie grins. Oka, the matriarch, is lying on her platform, still sound asleep. Unusual. She is the first one up in the morning. Oka, a zoo favorite with keepers and visitors, at thirty-eight, is the second-oldest gorilla in captivity. Arriving from Africa in 1941, with her even disposition and amusing antics, she quickly won everyone over. This year she enjoyed a winter game of pelting visitors with snowballs from her outside cage. They loved it. Just yesterday, a man had asked Howie if they still had Oka. He

Mwasi is subdued.

Knox-Sullivan
Bookmobile

had seen her twenty years ago as a boy and never fogotten her.

"Hey, Oka," Howie says. "Up and at 'em. Time for break-fast!"

No response.

Howie goes into Oka's cage and nudges her. She doesn't respond. She is cold.

Tears spring into Howie's eyes. She has died in her sleep. He will have to report this immediately to the veterinarian and to the curator, Jim Doherty, who also is fond of Oka. Only yesterday Oka seemed lethargic, wasn't eating properly. Doherty himself went to the cafeteria and bought her five different kinds of soft drinks and three pieces of cinnamon toast to tempt her appetite. Oka affected people that way.

8 A.M.

Two climbers and pruners work on trees between the eagle aviary and the wild-horse range, busily trimming overgrowth and removing dead branches.

Without warning, a bird with a ten-foot wingspan hurls through the trees, striking Frank Kerr on the shoulder. Completely surprised, he drops his pruning knife and shouts.

The bird is a fright; black, its bare head and neck are dark gray and wrinkled and it has a collar of fluffy white feathers. It vanishes into the trees.

One pruner runs to telephone for help.

Again the bird flies out of the trees at Kerr. He flails his arms, fighting it off.

In less than ten minutes Assistant Superintendent of the World of Birds Eric Edler and Keeper Robert Edington arrive with a net. They go into the woods and emerge in five minutes with the bird. It is the twenty-pound Miss McNasty, an Andean Condor, escaped from her cage.

8:30 A.M.

D R. EMIL DOLENSEK is sad as he starts his morning rounds. He had just examined Oka and discovered that she died of a coronary. He is grateful that she didn't have to suffer. He will miss Oka. She seemed to understand that he was her doctor and didn't scream and hoot at him the way other gorillas did when he had to treat them for various rheumatic diseases.

As he drives the animal ambulance to the shorebird exhibit, the doctor thinks of something that makes him smile. Good— he can use it; the morning has begun grimly. What he remembers is a recent grand-rounds lecture at Yale, the audience including all of the clinicians at the university. Dolensek, introduced as "Doctor," not D.V.M., talked about a case he was working on, a male from the Bronx.

The patient was born in East Africa, came to the United States at age one and a half. Now, at age twenty-three, he weighs 450 pounds, is slightly over five feet tall, has black skin and an abundance of black body hair. Dolensek then went through the entire medical history. At the end of his lecture he showed slides of the patient. Completely surprised, the assemblage of doctors roared with laughter at the lowland gorilla.

Dolensek is still chuckling as he pulls up before the bird exhibit. Senior Keeper James Bardsley is waiting. He is worried about one leg of a black-winged stilt. It seems malformed and the bird has some trouble walking. The doctor examines it carefully, watches it walk, suggests a diet heavy in calcium, and decides that the abnormality is congenital. The keeper then asks him to look at a black swan that had been hit with a stone, then seemed all right, but now staggers when it walks and occasionally falls. Dolensek watches the swan for ten minutes; then, as the keeper holds it, he takes a blood sample, injects it with an anti-inflammatory drug and an antibiotic, and asks the keeper to isolate the swan and watch it carefully.

Then he gets into his ambulance and drives to the World of Birds to look at a tinamou with an abscessed head. Emil Dolensek is widely respected at the zoo. Young, soft-spoken, self-assured, dedicated, he gave up a lucrative private practice in Connecticut to accept the challenge of being zoo doctor with about 3,500 patients. His approach to his work and

Dr. Emil Dolensek and a two-week-old baby emu

his personality make him get involved before the patient becomes ill, and he has a strong belief that the zoo must have concerned, responsible keepers looking after the animals and birds. His own involvement is complete as he sees animals born here, watches them grow, and gets to know at last two or three generations of most species.

Once, asked what it was like to be the doctor for one of the world's great zoos, he said, "The hardest thing is the responsibility. Every time I handle an animal I'm causing it distress—discomfort, fright, pain, perhaps even death. I always hope I'm right to do it, but sometimes I'm wrong."

8:40 A.M.

JAMES DOHERTY and a keeper stand looking in the wild-boar enclosure. A powerful sow, sleek as a sheet of steel, stares belligerently at them, fierce little eyes agleam. Beside her, two small wild piglets follow her as she moves. Twice, using her snout, she thrusts them violently aside. The little boars stagger, nearly fall.

"How long has this been going on?" Doherty asks.

"I'm not sure," the keeper says. "But it looks like she's rejecting them. Hasn't let them suckle in several hours."

"Let's not take any more chances," the curator says. "Give the little guys to Susan at Children's Zoo. She'll take better care of them than their mother ever could."

Rejected or undernourished animals often are placed in the Children's Zoo, where the staff of women nurse them to health and normal activity. Yesterday a rejected axis-deer fawn was taken there.

9 A.M.

THIS is the day of the weekly 2 P.M. zoo parade of animals and birds from the Children's Zoo. Margaret, Brett, Joanna, and Allison are at the riding track readying two dromedary camels, Ginger and Cindy. They have buckets of soapy and clear water; they scrub the camels vigorously, then rinse them. The animals blink their eyes at the young women and look down their noses contemptuously, as only camels can. One of them sighs, "I swear they make you feel like they're doing you a big favor!"

9:05 A.M.

THE Reptile House. A shipment arrives from an animal dealer. As usual, Superintendent Peter Brazaitis insists upon opening it. He is cautious, doesn't have complete faith in animal dealers. This is a wooden box, with the new arrival inside, in a cloth bag. The label on the bag reads MONITOR LIZARD.

"I'll handle it, Pete," one of the three keepers, who has been here only six months, says. "It's only a lizard."

Brazaitis shakes his head. Carefully, he places the bag in a close-meshed snake cage, unties the neck, gingerly opens it with a long broom handle, then closes the cage door.

Out slithers not a harmless lizard but a large, deadly black mamba.

The keeper pales. Brazaitis, his point made, says nothing.

9:15 A.M.

THE old copper roof of the Elephant House, rusted green, shines like jade in the clear morning light. Three young Asian elephants in the outside moat play an old pachyderm

A "frieze" of elephants outside the Elephant House

: 36

game of grab-tail, snatching one another's tails with their trunks and hanging on. They look like a frieze from an ancient Hindu temple come alive.

Inside this most famous building at the zoo, although sunlight is streaming in, it is still dim. Shadows lie in corners and the elephants trumpet annoyed sounds through their trunks, like grumpy old men being awakened too early.

Dennis Cornax switches on the wall lights before he sweeps out Cutie's stall. He hopes she feels better this morning. She hasn't been eating, is irritable, which is unlike her. He smiles, remembering how Cutie treated him when he started as a keeper. As he would enter her stall, she'd reach over with her trunk, take the broom from him, and wave it playfully. Then she'd drop it; he'd pick it up, and she would grab it again. In about ten minutes she would stop playing and permit him to sweep out her area.

Cutie is in the far corner of her stall. Cornax opens the door and steps in. Cuties rushes, swings her trunk like a club, hits him with such force that he strikes his head against the concrete wall near the door. He falls out through the door, unconscious, head gushing blood.

Hearing him fall, Senior Keeper Warren Lawston runs from the office to help Cornax. He closes Cutie's door, phones the telephone operator for an ambulance. Within thirty minutes Cornax is in Fordham Hospital. He has a concussion; it takes five stitches to close his head wound. His first words: "Cutie's my friend. She's sick."

9:25 A.M.

SENIOR Superintendent Andy Winnegar stands by as two keepers prepare two shipments of birds, four young rheas and four tinamous, that will be crated and shipped by air to Santo Domingo.

The Bronx Zoo currently has 85 birds, 16 animals, and 6 reptiles on breeding loan to other collections. In a two-year period the zoo bred 161 mammals, 304 birds, 77 reptiles and amphibians, and also loaned, traded, or sold 334 animals from its surplus, graphically proving Director Conway's operating theory that his zoo is acting as a replenishing repository for wild animals, especially vanishing species.

Winnegar, who misses no detail in his World of Birds, watches until the last nail is hammered into the shipping crates.

9:35 A.M.

JAMES DOHERTY stands at Wolf Woods, watching Brutus, Coal, Cleo, and Buster. The curator had started his rounds of the mammal installations some time ago, had helped get Cornax into the ambulance, worries about him, but now stands at a favorite place for morning visits. Wolves still hold

Portrait of a tundra wolf

a mystique for him. It is difficult to see them among the rocks and foliage, and he is pleased that he works with a director who believes in natural habitats that exhibit *how* animals live. Now he sees the wolves, stretched on the ground, heads raised, watching him. The black wolf, Coal, again reminds him that the learning process in a zoo never ends.

Until Coal and Brutus bred, he wasn't certain which animals were dominant, which wolves ruled. Doherty knew that these remarkable animals practiced not only the survival-of-the-fittest theory but birth control as well. Only the strongest of the males and females breed. With the breeding of Coal began the harassment of Cleo. Not only did Coal keep Cleo away from the other males; she wouldn't let her eat. Finally, the keeper had to feed Cleo by herself. Doherty wasn't surprised to discover that the males sided with the dominant female, which meant that Cleo would never bear young.

Sometime after the cubs—one male and two females—were born, Doherty was pleased to see that Cleo was permitted to carry food into the den for them. The males also fed the cubs. Doherty was pleased, again, when after a two-day rainstorm flooded the den, Cleo brought one cub out of the den. Coal, the mother, brought two. Both wolves cuddled the young under bushes to keep them warm. When the rain stopped and the den was again dry, Coal trotted over and retrieved her cub from Cleo, now the cubs' respected aunt.

9:40 A.M.

THE man's actions are suspicious. He sneaks behind a growth of bushes, gets on his knees, and inspects a hidden object. This is Joe Ruf, retired senior keeper, checking his trapline. He traps creatures that plague the zoo—rats, pigeons, wild foxes, feral cats. Rats and pigeons eat the food in the aviaries; wild foxes and cats attack the sleeping birds. Stray dogs are dreaded. They are controlled, mainly, with the Cap-Chur tranquilizer pistol, then given to the S.P.C.A.

Ruf's problem today will be a huge flock of city pigeons that have flown in for zoo welfare.

9:45 A.M.

ON Mark MacNamara's belt the two-way radio crackles an emergency as he rides his electric cart, making his own early-morning check of mammals. He has just looked at a young male hartebeest that was chased into a wire fence by an aggressive female and broke its left horn. With the help of Ray Deiter, the assistant veterinarian, Mark tried to get the animal into a smaller enclosure, away from the females, but couldn't because the injured animal was too frightened. So he rounded up the females on the four-acre exhibit, removed them from the area, and left Deiter tranquilizing the hartebeest and attempting to stop the bleeding.

Now, listening to the urgent voice on the radio, Mark alerts Supervisor Fred Sterling at the Lion House, asking him to join him at the wisent range immediately.

He is concerned. The wisent is a European bison. It is extinct in the wild, and only a few exist in zoos. When Mark arrives at the range, Sterling is there.

Jackson's hartebeests

A large tree has been uprooted by the fighting bison. From their separate range, the female wisents crowd against the fence, watching the two sparring bulls.

Two keepers approach Mark. Sterling studies the situation as the animals charge, smash together, the smaller bull staggering, almost falling.

"He's had it," one keeper says. "If we don't stop this, I think that big bull will kill him."

The bulls originally were separated, but somehow a gate was left ajar, and the large bull entered and immediately charged the small one.

Female wisents, Norma and Necessity, watch the bulls battle.

"What do you think, Fred?" Mark says.

"Touchy," Sterling replies. "If we go in now, that big guy is so enraged he'll charge anything he sees."

Mark instructs the keepers to place plenty of grain in the corral with the females and to leave their gate open. He hopes that when the females begin noisily to eat, they'll attract the bulls, and perhaps one will join them.

At first it doesn't work. The smaller bull is over against the fence, bracing himself, obviously exhausted. The big bull stands glaring. Finally his ears twitch; he wheels around and trots through the gate, joining the females. Quickly, a keeper closes the gate.

"Radio the vet," Mark tells the other keeper. "That small bull is going to need some patching up."

The radio on his belt crackles again. It is zoo security—Joe Spadafino. He has observed that two fighting mouflon—wild sheep—have locked horns. When MacNamara and Sterling arrive at the wild-sheep range, the males are standing head to head, curved horns securely locked, holding them immobile. Mark and Fred maneuver the animals' heads to disengage the horns. Sterling slaps one of the wild sheep on the flank, sending it up the rocky hill behind them.

He is proud of what has been accomplished here, with these vanishing wild sheep, reduced to mere remnants living high in the rocky mountains of Sardinia and Corsica. In perfectly reproduced habitat, in a two-year period, the zoo has successfully raised 151 lambs.

*The Amazonian tiger bittern is an egg-breaker that adds hours to zoo workers'
tasks.*

9:50 A.M.

THE Aquatic Birds Building. A keeper catches an Amazonian
tiger bittern and engages in a task that none of the keepers
appreciates. The bittern has eaten its usual quota of fish several

hours ago. It is now the keeper's job to make the bird disgorge part of its meal. He does it by a skillful manipulation of stomach and throat until the bird regurgitates about half a cup of a foul-smelling mass.

This action is necessary because the pair of bitterns break their eggs and the intact fertile ones must be placed in an incubator in the World of Birds. When feeding their young, bitterns regurgitate part of their partially digested food directly into the bills of the chicks.

For two weeks keepers will have to collect this odious fish, and hand feed the newly hatched bitterns.

10 A.M.

GLEAMING like Inca gold in the bold summer light, the great bronze "Rainey Memorial Gates," a New York City landmark, are about to be opened. There are three other entrances to the zoo besides this main one, on Fordham Road, that attracts most visitors, many coming just to view the gates created by noted sculptor Paul Manship in 1934 and forged in Belgium. Flanked by pink granite lodgegates, the gates' impressive sculpture represents the animal kingdom, with everything from a lion to a tortoise.

Gatekeeper is slender, dark John Siciliano. Punctual, he starts to swing one gate open. This is a purely manual operation, with no electronic assistance swinging wide these massive, medieval-looking polished portals.

As Siciliano has one gate partially open, he sees motion inside the zoo grounds. Staring at him is a brown aoudad—or Barbary sheep, native to the mountains of North Africa—horns flared, long streamers of hair on throat, chest, and front legs. It dances backward, then tries to dart through the gate.

Siciliano closes the gate, waves his arms at the wild sheep, tries to drive it away from the entrance.

In one fast, balletlike movement, the sheep leaps the concrete wall that abuts the Bronx River. Landing twenty feet below in a bouncing, rubber-ball motion, the sheep quickly swims the river and runs straight ahead along the bank.

Siciliano alerts the Mammal Department. Now he opens the gates. Waiting are three regulars: Henry Frege, who has been coming to the zoo for fifty years and knows every animal by name, age and weight; Salomon Kubetz, who has been at the gate every morning for fifty-three years; and a newcomer, Angelo Calatena, who has visited every day for only a decade.

Seeing the gatekeeper somewhat flustered—unusual with the calm Siciliano—they ask what's wrong. He tells them, and the three assure him that the men from the Mammal Department are so good that they'll have the animal back in no time. Even as they talk, three keepers arrive with ropes and nets, get Siciliano's report, hurry below to the river, and begin their search for the traveling aoudad.

10:20 A.M.

THIRTY-ONE-YEAR-OLD Richard Lattis, assistant curator of education, overseer of the Children's Zoo, approaches the director's office in the Administration Building with mixed emotions. The Kentuckian hopes that he will be convincing. He knows that the director is aware of much of what he is going to present. But he also knows that this busy man has to juggle so many problems and pressing, day-by-day details that it is a good idea to refresh his memory. Lattis wants to enlarge the Children's Zoo; more space is badly needed. But money, as always, is tight, so he wants to put together a proposition to offer to the organizations and individuals who support the zoo.

William Conway awaits at his desk. Lattis is barely seated when he begins. "Bill," he says, "I know you're aware of all this, but I'm hoping we can get moving on a new Children's Zoo, and I'm here to give the project a shove."

Conway smiles, says go ahead, shove. He has his own pet projects, such as "Wild Asia," which he will be explaining to a foreign visitor today, and is sympathetic.

"First," Lattis says, "we're archaic. The Bronx Children's Zoo, built in 1941 as a temporary facility, was the first in this country. We've led the way in developing new methods of presenting animals to children. In the past ten years over three-point-two million visitors have passed through our tiny one-third-of-an acre site. Each day of our short seven-month season sees approximately three thousand visitors. But animals, exhibits, graphics, and learning space are squeezed and stressed to their limits."

Lattis gives Conway some quick verbal vignettes of what he has in mind for his new zoo for children: At one moment the child will creep through a forest. At "The Treetops," he will discover gibbons swinging through the trees. For a comparison, he can try his skill traversing a rope stretched between two poles. In this way he learns that he is different from a gibbon, which can easily do the feat, but similar in many respects, as he uses many of the same motions.

Then the child finds himself on a boardwalk, crossing the marsh inhabited by muskrats and raccoons as well as by ducks, frogs, turtles, and wading birds. This habitat will be particularly useful for introducing the concept of the predator-prey-scavenger relationship.

At the pond the child can compare swimming techniques among ducks, fishes, and turtles. Why do aquatic turtles have webs of skin between their toes, whereas box turtles do not? With proper supervision, the child will pick up a small turtle to see how hard the shell is and how the turtle moves its head and legs. The bottom of the pond will be partly exposed, to reveal through glass the rare sight of turtles walking along the bottom of the pond.

An extreme change in habitat comes with the desert; this will present a totally different environment to the New

Yorker. Emphasis will be placed on the necessity of conservation of water and of escape from the torturous rays of the sun.

What more appropriate animal to learn from than the well-known, so-called "prairie dog"? This animal is not a dog at all, but a pleasant little rodent of the Western United States. The child will walk or crawl through a child-sized prairie-dog burrow system that dovetails with a real prairie-dog burrow. Much of the prairie dog's tunnel system can be exposed by replacing the roof with glass. The child can encounter the prairie dog's sleeping den, food storage area, and escape tunnel. He or she can see what sorts of food the animal eats, how it digs new tunnels. . . .

New acquaintances at the Children's Zoo

Laughing, Conway holds up a hand. "Enough. Put this all together in a formal presentation and we'll see what we can do."

10:58 A.M.

Sᴇᴛ in almost brooding isolation on a rocky ledge, the bat-black exterior of the cubical buildings of the World of Darkness immediately establishes a tone of the drama and the mystery of night, when, unknown to most of us, sixty percent of the world's land vertebrates are active.

It is an exhibit unique in the world of zoos, and it has taken much study on the part of the zoo's staff successfully to reverse the life-style of the denizens of the dark so that they can live normally and reproduce here, in their eerie world.

Inside, bright lights have been off for twenty-eight minutes. Lights are on from 10 ᴘ.ᴍ. to 10 ᴀ.ᴍ., so that the night creatures can sleep as they do in their normal daylight world. Then the dim blue and red lights are switched on, simulating pale moonlight, and the animals, birds, and reptiles begin moving.

Visitors enter the ghostly world almost timorously, hearing a whippoorwill calling; far away, a bull alligator roaring. Still farther away an owl hoots, a frog chorus crescendos, and a kit fox howls shrilly. The sounds are taped, but they are very real, as they were recorded in the wild. They are not overwhelming, however, as the various calls and sounds are loud only in front of the exhibit from which they emanate.

People move slowly, uncertainly, through this shadow world; one man whispers, "We need a guide," but groups follow one another through the thirty major displays, the exhibits divided into three halls: the Forest After Dark, Wings in the Night, and Refuge Underground.

Senior Keeper Cosmo Barbetto has just fed the four vampire bats fresh beef blood, which he obtains from a slaughterhouse. The bats need a half gallon a week.

Now Barbetto goes into the most spectacular display, the bat cave, which is copied from settings in Trinidad, realistically created from fiberglass, as are so many of the zoo's displays.

People gasp; one woman makes a frightened little shriek as Cosmo stirs up the bats and about two hundred of them begin flitting about over his head.

11 A.M.

CHECKING his watch, Cosmo abruptly leaves the bat cave and goes to Wings in the Night's thirty-foot demonstration area. People wait before it for the eleven-o'clock demonstration. Here, several Indian fruit bats, the world's largest bats, are in the air, their five-foot wingspread producing a continual rising whisper of sound. Cosmo raises his

right arm. One great bat swoops, lands on his arm, clinging there while visitors express horror. Cosmo talks about bats, silly superstitions, and false beliefs.

The visitors leave the dim blue world, blinking at the summer sunlight. Still in the clutch of that strange world of night, few talk as they walk away.

11:10 A.M.

THE Children's Zoo. Children, varying in age from two to ten, are in groups around the "contact" area. They touch and talk to six Barbados sheep; eight goats; Jerry, the Sicilian donkey; a baby antelope; and various species of rabbits, geese, and chickens. The children are well behaved, owing more to fascination than to the watchful eyes of their parents.

Operations Supervisor Susan Basford is also watching, careful that there is no rough handling of her charges. As she stands looking at a five-year-old attempting to get close enough to a goat to nuzzle it, a man rushes up, a white Pekin duck struggling in his arms.

"Don't you supervise your birds?" he says. "This one was trying to drown another one in the duck pond!"

Gently, Susan explains that this is the mating season. Amused, the man hands her the duck and apologizes. "I hope I haven't upset anything," he says with an embarrassed laugh.

An Indian fruit bat hangs in its favorite position.   : 55

11:15 A.M.

THE Ape House. An overweight woman in tight trousers, a small girl beside her, stands inside the building looking at a mirror. A sign above the mirror reads, "You are looking at the most dangerous predator on earth."

The woman, indignant, starts to splutter. Her daughter says, "What's the matter, Mom? What does 'predator' mean?"

11:18 A.M.

NICOLAS GILENO is twenty-three years old; he is slender and short, and looks fifteen. He always wanted to be a jockey, and as a boy he worked in a stable at a racetrack. He likes to be around animals, so he works here, at the cafeteria, as a sweeper. Routinely, he puts his broom away and quietly leaves the cafeteria for fifteen minutes at this hour every day.

He walks quickly to the Lion House. As he approaches the first outside cage, he slows down, then stops, waiting for Darky, the female puma, to see him. She does, instantly crouching and staring at him. There are three men and two women standing before the cougar's cage. They turn their heads to see what attracts the cat. It had been completely oblivious of them. Now the cat has come vibrantly alive, eyes gleaming, tail switching.

William Conway, the general director

Timing his move dramatically, Nick Gileno saunters toward the puma. As he approaches, the cat bounds toward him, purring loudly.

Nick Gileno repeats his performance, walking to the opposite side of the cage. The cat again bounds after him. "She loves me!" Nick says aloud to everyone and to no one. Nick does it once more. The cat responds. The people stare, astonished. Proudly, Nick walks back to the cafeteria, Darky, the puma, nose against the bars, watches him go.

Watching from an electric cart is the slim, dark-haired director, William Conway, who knows every animal, as well

as every employee, at his zoo. He enters his observation of Nick and the puma in a notebook he carries to record animal behavior, and wonders about the magnetism some people hold for animals. This puma, he knows, is inscrutable, never evinces interest in anything except food. Conway reminds himself happily that the learning process in the zoo goes on forever.

11:20 A.M.

THE telephone rings in the office of the curator of reptiles, interrupting John Behler, who is studying a report of the effectiveness of the electrical installation devised to alleviate animal losses due to mechanical failures at the Reptile House. A monitoring panel now provides electronic surveillance of the enclosures and of the heating and cooling systems, and will signal an alarm when the malfunction occurs.

The caller asks Behler if he is in charge of the reptile department. When the caller learns that he is, the man identifies himself as Timothy Warke, calling from his apartment in Elmhurst, Queens. "I have an adult South American anaconda," Warke says. "Friendly, healthy, ten feet long. I'd like to donate him to the zoo."

Behler wants to know how long he has had it. Three years. Why does he want to give it away? Family matter.

The zoo is offered about a thousand snakes a year, often problem snakes—ailing, ill-tempered, or both. Few are accepted. But the anaconda sounds interesting, and they can use a good male. Behler immediately will send someone to pick it up. He phones Pete Brazaitis at the House of Reptiles, tells him to take Bob Brandner with him and get the snake. If his two experts like it, the anaconda will be quarantined and studied at length before it is placed on exhibit.

——— *11:25 A.M.* ———

Two Australian sailors enter the World of Birds; one reads aloud from wall signs: "Birds are warm-blooded, egg-laying, toothless vertebrates, specialized for flight. If an animal has feathers, it's a bird; if it hasn't, it isn't."

His companion reads aloud another sign: "Birds evolved at least 150,000,000 years ago. Today there are 8,600 species."

As they stand before the Australian Outback exhibit they become solemn. The wind-eroded red sandstone, the stunted trees, give the exhibit the desolate look of a desert. " 'Orrible!" one says. "Yeah, matey," the other Australian chuckles. "Just like it is."

Overhearing them, Curator Donald Bruning feels good about the remark. He strives constantly to keep all exhibits realistically alive. The thirty-three-year-old Bruning, an expert on South American Darwin rheas, has received his doctorate as a result of his in-depth study of the birds here at the zoo. He personally raised twenty-two, the largest number ever raised in captivity, and is so successful that the zoo has sent sixty of the rheas to other zoos and erased the possibility of this rare bird's ever becoming extinct.

Bruning has been here six times so far today, and has just come into the World of Birds from Propagation One, an off-exhibit breeding compound behind this main building. Here rare and endangered birds are bred and housed; the pride of the zoo are the very rare Malayan and Palawan peacock pheasants. Bruning has just examined a clutch of eggs from the Palawans. He started with one pair of the birds, and so far

twenty-three young have been produced. With his two pairs of Malayans he has raised fourteen to date and is pleased that this is the only zoo in the United States to breed them successfully.

Now Bruning is carefully checking all exhibits to determine what trimming is needed and which exhibits need new trees and foliage. He depends heavily upon Assistant Superintendent Eric Edler, whose specialty this is, but he also likes to make frequent spot checks himself.

Bruning stops at the African Rain Forest. On a huge tree, a vine of the Acanthus family, bearing bright blue flowers, is attached to a wild grapevine which gives it support, enabling it to grow to the top of the tree. He picks up some fallen blue flowers, which he will give to the satin bower bird to decorate its bower.

The tree is Bruning's pride. With a girth of eight feet, it is forty feet high and has six long limbs reaching to the ceiling. Bruning smiles now, remembering Assistant Curator of Exhibits John Calvin Sutton's twisting the poet's words when he referred to this tree. "Only God can make a tree," Sutton said, "economically." This tree took Sutton and four men one month, working eight hours a day, to make, at a cost of $20,000.

This man-made masterpiece required two and one half tons of material. Limbs were prefabricated, constructed of reinforcing steel rods, then covered with black hardware-cloth wire. Using block and tackle and ladders, workmen welded

These emus enjoy their outside enclosure.

the limbs to the ceiling, and covered them with fiberglass cloth permeated with resin. Then this was spread with a heavy paste of fiberglass resin, colored to look like bark. Bark from a Spanish cork tree was then embedded in the resin paste, placed carefully to follow the lateral growth line of the tree. The limbs were then married to the trunk, also made of steel rods, fiberglass, and resin and covered with natural cork bark. If kept moist, that bark will last for fifteen years.

This most unusual tree was also constructed to contain copper tubes to carry water to the live plants planted in it. A misting system waters the plants once a day.

Bruning likes to startle visitors with the story of the tree, and of the spectacular cliffs in the New World Rain Forest, which were also made by Sutton. He first got permission to take a cast of New Jersey's famous rock formation the Palisades. Casts of latex rubber, thirty feet high and forty long, took four men one month to make. All the men got massive cases of poison ivy while cleaning the rock face.

Fiberglass rocks were made from the rubber molds. Then, in the World of Birds, a steel frame, forty feet high and sixty feet around the curve, was covered with wire mesh and paper backing, then sprayed with liquid cement. The fiberglass rock was welded to the frame; liquid cement was again sprayed in certain areas, so natural vegetation could grow, as it will not grow on fiberglass.

Result: Tree and cliff look so real that it is difficult to convince viewers that they are not.

THUNDER rumbles in the Reptile House; lightning crackles; rain falls. Visitors stand entranced. They know the hours of the thunderstorms and complain if they don't occur on time.

When the rain stops, Senior Keeper Bob Brandner takes a mackerel from a bucket and throws it to a crocodile. As is customary, the crocodile picks it up, snaps it quickly before swallowing it. Half of the fish breaks off, flies across the barrier, and strikes a woman visitor squarely in the face.

It is Bob Brandner's mother-in-law, who has come to see how her son-in-law makes a living.

Brandner is delighted when he is called by Brazaitis to accompany him on the errand to Queens to get the anaconda. He hurries from the Reptile House to get the truck.

THE phone rings in the office of F. Wayne King, director of zoology and conservation for the New York Zoological Society. Although he is headquartered at the Bronx Zoo, is an assistant to the director, and is the person to whom all the

A Burmese python

curators are responsible, many of Dr. King's activities are worldwide. This call is from the World Wildlife Fund, in Washington, D.C., asking if the Zoological Society will help fund a National Park in Costa Rica. "Will you contribute to buying the land?" the caller asks.

Dr. King says he will query the Society. One of the busiest men at the zoo, he keeps the conversation short. Not only does he serve as a committee member of the International Union for the Conservation of Nature, in Morges, Switzerland, but he was one of the moving forces behind the passing of the

United States Endangered Species Act, which prohibits the importation of tiger and leopard skins and those other endangered animals. He also keeps in constant touch with the Zoological Society's far-flung programs of conservation in the field, ranging from Angola to Papua, New Guinea.

Right now he is hard at work on his speech for the "Wild-

A California king snake

Knox-Sullivan
Bookmobile

life in America" symposium in Washington, D.C., where he will lecture on the wildlife trade and how it continues to endanger animals. From his chair at the Bronx Zoo, Dr. King reaches out to save wildlife everywhere.

───── *11:55 A.M.* ─────

THE three-car, sixty-nine-passenger Safari Train that begins its tour at the Elephant House completes the first half of its forty-five-minute trip. Rusty, a college student, one of the summer drivers, talks as he takes the tractor train over the eleven miles of twisting roads.

His words drift back from the sound system to people walking behind the train. "Just ahead and to the right are the Père David, rarest of all deer, completely extinct in the wild for at least seventy years. Rarer than Rembrandts, they are extinct in nature just as the dinosaur is.

"Originally, they inhabited swampy areas of northern China. There are now several hundred of these deer, found only in zoos. Our herd is the largest of the Western Hemisphere. This species would not exist today if the Duke of Bedford had not brought a few from China to his estate, Woburn Abbey, in England, about 1900.

"In the next exhibit are the Przewalski wild horses, the only true wild horses living today; just a few may still roam in the wilderness of western Mongolia, but even this is uncer-

The Père David deer, rarest of all deer

tain. There are only two hundred fifty left in the world. They
are the most valuable animals in this zoo. Though this horse
is a relative of our domestic horse, it is not its ancestor. It is
a truly wild animal, never domesticated by man."

Rusty usually makes a few witty asides that aren't in the
copy prepared by the zoo, but today he stays with the script.

Knox-Sullivan
Bookmobile

Noon

VISITORS line up at the long cafeteria counter, laughing and enjoying themselves, happy with what they've seen of the zoo and with the lunch to come.

One woman isn't too happy. She scowls and orders two cups of coffee, saying loudly that one is for her husband, who is coming by helicopter to join her. She sits at a table, looking at her watch; then finally she hurls one cup of coffee to the floor.

James Joy, one of the three unit managers at the cafeteria, tries to calm her. He has been at the zoo for thirty-nine years and is adept at handling such situations. But he fails, and sends for help. The woman, obviously hysterical, is finally taken away in an ambulance. The zoo's security and communication systems are so effective, the entire action takes barely fifteen minutes.

Security Officer Joe Spadafino, who arrives to assist, does a double take at a scene at a luncheon table. A young man passes a bottle of orange and a straw to his companion. The companion, dressed in short pants, a red golf shirt and a white sailor's hat, is a chimpanzee.

Amused, Spadafino shakes his head. One hour ago he was called to evict a man who had gathered a crowd around him. The man was carrying a huge boa constrictor wrapped around his upper torso.

The uniformed Spadafino strolls over to the cafeteria table, stands and looks calmly at the man and the chimpanzee. "You're supposed to come to look at the animals that are here, not bring your own. It isn't permitted."

Without argument, the man rises, takes his chimpanzee by the hand, and leaves.

1 P.M.

CHILDREN'S Zoo. A young schoolteacher with her class of twenty stands before a camel. "That hump," she says, "is full of water. This ship of the desert can go for weeks without drinking."

Walking to the pen of the Barbados sheep, she points to one and continues with her misinformation. "That female is called a hughey; the small ones, little hughies."

Not far away, at the Elephant House, attractive brunette Judy Enis will be more accurate with the zoo information she passes on to the sixteen children she has on tour. She is the chairwoman of "Friends of the Zoo," three hundred volunteers trained by curators and by the zoo's education department. Working during the week, and even during weekends, upon request, Friends of the Zoo acts as guide for many groups, not only of schoolchildren but of senior citizens, retarded children, and foreign visitors. A valuable adjunct to the busy zoo staff, members of the group donate their time because they enthusiastically believe that the zoo is a valuable educational tool for the preservation and protection of our rapidly vanishing wild animals.

1:30 P.M.

IN the kitchen of the World of Birds, pretty young Dorma Collins takes a tray of white mice from the freezer to feed the owls and the frogmouths. She thinks the mice look like they are sleeping, and supposes the birds must think the same thing.

1:40 P.M.

BEAR Den. Snowball, the only polar bear born and raised in New York City, is having a first birthday party. The famous offspring of Olga and Ivan stands near the arctic pool, spotless silky white hair and glowing dark eyes making the little bear look like an animated child's toy as he moves toward the birthday cake. The cake, made by Senior Keeper Frank Casella, is mackerel and whipped cream.

The press is here with cameras, television sound equipment, lights, and hubbub. Spectators stand and stare.

As Snowball approaches the cake, mother Olga moves

A great horned owl

protectively forward. To distract her, so the camera can have
a clear view of the little bear taking the first bite of his cake,
Frank Casella throws Olga some apples, which she loves.

"You're not supposed to do that!" a spectator shouts at
Frank. "There are signs all over the place: DON'T FEED THE
ANIMALS!"

Frank explains who he is and why he threw the apples, and the visitor grins and joins in, clapping his hands and singing "Happy Birthday" as the little white bear takes a big bite of the cake. Everyone laughs at the whipped cream on Snowball's nose.

1:50 *P.M.*

DIM blue light. Moonlight. Cosmo Barbetto, senior keeper at the World of Darkness, enjoys a daily ritual. He soaks a loaf of Italian bread, which he buys every morning on Arthur Avenue, in the Italian section of the Bronx, in water and feeds it to the strange two-toed sloth. The animal also likes apples and bananas, but this bread is its favorite food. It hangs upside down in a tree in the man-made twilight, inanimate as a bruised branch.

Cosmo, built like a Japanese sumo wrestler, a kind and gentle man, mourns for the sloth, for its ugliness and its zombielike movements, and wonders what nature ever intended for such an animal. He has strong sympathy for his creatures of the dark, one reason his world is so seductive to visitors.

2 *P.M.*

THE parade starts promptly; the fifteen zoo-employee participants line up in front of the Children's Zoo. A twelve-year-old boy whose mother works at the zoo drapes a boa constrictor around his upper torso. The arm-thick snake raises its head, flicks its tongue.

Olga loves apples.

Parade master is vivacious, dark-haired Jill Murphy, who supervises the Riding Track. She rides in an Amish spring wagon pulled by Kanga, the Norwegian fjord pony, behind two very clean camels that lead. In the back of the wagon is a portable sound system that blares a rousing parade march. Two ponies pull two carts, followed by a Sicilian donkey, a baby llama, an Australian white goose, a wild boar on a leash, a Pygmy horse, two goats, a peacock, and two chickens.

Everyone has a colored balloon that floats from a long string. The parade moves briskly, noisily; children stare open-mouthed, leave their parents and follow. The parade will halt in half an hour at the Sea Lion Pool so visitors can have a close-up view of the animals and can ask questions.

2:03 P.M.

THE World of Birds. Electric lights are on from 6 A.M. to 6 P.M., to give the birds the normal twelve hours of daylight. Now the lights dim. It thunders. There are intermittent flashes of lightning, then the drizzle of rain on leaves in Asia, the Forest Edge.

Eric Edler, the young, blond-haired assistant superintendent, is studying the background display as a woman visitor walks up to him. She looks at her watch. "You are three minutes late with the thunderstorm."

Cindy, ready for the parade

As Edler apologizes, Dr. Donald Bruning arrives. He grins at Edler. "We better shape up!" Then Bruning goes off to the New World Rain Forest.

The rain stops; an exotic sun bird sits on a branch, wings spread like a huge butterfly, drying them. A shama thrush darts from tree to tree.

Asia, the Forest Edge is skylighted, but there is still not enough sun for plants to develop fully. They tend to get "leggy." Edler is working on a way to solve that problem, and he is aware, too, that visitors can see the "soil" line against the background wall, even though it has realistic foliage painted on it. For him, this gives a feeling of confinement. A perfectionist, he considers positioning a cherry-tree-trunk section and roots against the wall. Planting passion flowers in the log will hide the wall line and give a natural look. He approves of the log he already has cunningly placed diagonally in the forefront of the exhibit. This catches the visitor's eye and takes it right into the exhibit of exotic birds.

The constant replacing of the fauna and flora keeps Eric Edler on the move. For example, he goes to the meadowlands of New Jersey to search for Atlantic-white-cedar logs, which have a huge root system and last longer than most other trees in the exhibit.

Now he sees a sun bittern beginning to build a nest of Spanish moss. He makes a mental note to watch the bird. If she doesn't complete the nest, he will; he can do a better job of it than the bird can. He has constructed nests of twigs for

Eric Edler builds a nest a bird can't complete.

ibis, herons, and egrets. Edler has made more than twenty kinds of nests, including those woven to look exactly like the masterpieces the birds themselves make.

He chuckles to himself thinking about the time he even fooled the curator of birds. In a satin-bower-bird display, the male would not construct a bower to attract the female. So, one day, Edler made a perfect straw bower. When the curator saw it, he became very excited, saying it was the first time that a bower bird had ever built a nest in captivity. He sent Edler rushing to get a photographer to record the rare happening.

Pink flamingos and dalmation pelicans, zoo favorites

Walking over to the present satin-bower-bird exhibit, Edler studies the bird, thinking about it. The male uses blue objects to decorate its bower, where it lures the female for courtship. Keepers supply the bird with blue flowers, feathers, bits of glass and ceramic—anything blue—to give the bower bird something to work with.

Edler believes that he has made a discovery important to the bird world: He has noticed that the male bower bird not only decorates its bower cleverly but discards the flowers when they fade, the fruit when it decays, the feathers when they become discolored and bedraggled. Edler has determined that the bird possesses an aesthetic sense, something he has never seen or read about with any other species of bird.

2:30 P.M.

WILLIAM CONWAY stops his electric cart beside the Lion House. His guests are Dr. José Thomé, director of the Zoological and Botanical Foundation, Rio Grande del Sol, one of South America's largest zoos, and Dr. Thomé's interpreter. The State Department has arranged this brain-picking visit, and Conway is in his element, as he always is when talking of his zoo's accomplishments and its future plans.

He takes the two men into the basement of the Lion House, where surplus animals are housed, and shows them thirty unique deer that have the two visitors oohing and ahing. They are Malayan mouse deer, standing only twelve inches at the shoulder, long considered delicate and rare in captivity, until, as Conway explains, the Bronx Zoo kept one pair under red lights, reversing their day and night, which solved all problems. That pair bred so readily that the zoo had to donate some of the many offspring to other zoos.

In the electric cart Conway takes his guests to a high point overlooking the Bronx River. Sunlight glints on the narrow river as it snakes through the zoo grounds. From the shadows on the other side, gray shapes suddenly become rhinos plodding toward the viewers. In another area, elephants move single file through the trees. Animals are gradually being transferred from buildings, cages, and enclosures to this new area.

The elephants explore Wild Asia.

The general director points out the animals and explains that his zoo is gradually being organized into zoo-geographical areas, and that already Africa and South America are almost completed. He points across the river, and shocks his guests.

"There," he says, "we are going to put the visitors in cages and let tigers, leopards, elephants, great gaur, and other Asian animals and birds roam freely."

Dr. Thomé checks with his interpreter to see if he has translated correctly.

Conway says he will explain, and goes on to tell why his new project, "Wild Asia," is a special breakthrough for a city zoo. The project's forty acres make it as large as some entire zoos (such as the London and Philadelphia zoos), but the

Rhinos roam free in Wild Asia.

site also poses problems. Although it is thickly wooded, with outcroppings of rock, its entire length is bordered by the busy Bronx River Parkway, which offers unacceptable visual pollution for a zoo trying to present natural settings for its animals. Because the animals of Wild Asia are mostly from endangered species, Conway wants enough space to be able to propagate them in numbers for decades to come. He also wants to preserve as much of the park land as possible. Blasting for zoo moats would destroy too much of the natural setting.

"Thus," Conway says to the interpreter, "it became evident that we should cage the visitor within the animals' environment, rather than the other way around."

Much study proved this could be accomplished by using a one-sided conveyance, a monorail, which would eliminate the need for extensive excavation and also hide completely the parkway behind the backs of the visitors. The monorail, six trains with nine cars, each car holding ten passengers, will carry 1,620 people through Wild Asia in one hour, traveling 34 changes of levels. The cab of each train, such as the *Bengali Express* and the *Irawaddy Coaches*, will carry a trained lecturer. Each habitat in Wild Asia will have an appropriate name—South China Hills, Kanha Meadow, Tiger Machan, Hindu Kush.

Conway sits back, barraged with questions from Dr. Thomé.

2:40 P.M.

OUTSIDE the Lion House a group of young men stand before the cage of Igo, a 700-pound Siberian tiger, the largest of the world's cats. They clatter a stick against the bars of the cage, snarl and hiss, trying to irritate the tiger. When the cat finally roars at them angrily, eyes blazing, they move to the next cage, that of Mom, a Siberian female, and repeat the performance.

Robert Terracuso, young, dark-haired senior keeper at the Lion House, approaches them.

"Don't tease the tigers," he says softly. "They're caged. Isn't that enough?" Then he reaches out and gently touches the nose of Igo.

Sheepishly the agitators move off.

Terracuso stands staring after them, depressed by their actions. He will be glad when the Wild Asia open habitat area is completed and the cats are no longer caged.

A young woman and two children come breezing up to Igo's cage. "Hello, beautiful," she says cheerily to the tiger. "How are you today?" The children stare in admiration and awe.

Terracuso feels better. He goes inside the Lion House to look in on the two jaguars and the other tigers.

As usual, Dacca, the Bengal tiger, has taken the hose from the keeper attempting to clean her cage. The big cat pretends to let it go. The keeper yanks, but Dacca is feigning, and still has the hose. Terracuso sighs. It will take four keepers to play tug of war with Dacca before she releases the hose.

At the far end of the Lion House he sees that Juanita is also playing her usual baiting game. Terracuso wants to shout at the elderly woman walking up to the jaguar's cage, but knows it will only frighten everyone in the place. So he breaks into a fast walk. But not fast enough.

Juanita likes the toys children carry, such as monkeys on sticks; hats; dolls; ladies' handbags—especially handbags.

Her cunning technique is to attract the person with the object she wants by sticking one paw partway through the bars. As the visitor walks closer, she extends the paw just a bit more. When the person is close enough, Juanita suddenly whips her paw out and grabs the object she wants.

Terracuso sees her working her con game now with the woman idly swinging her small handbag. Juanita's timing is superb.

Fascinated by the magnificent cat that seems to be beckoning with her paw, the woman walks closer. When she is within striking distance, out flashes Juanita's paw, snatching the bag.

The woman stands stunned; then, seeing Terracuso approaching, she is amused. "Your cat has my bag. With money she can't spend."

Terracuso's second-in-command, Richard Kiggings, comes sauntering up, tells the woman that the cat never harms the handbags. In a matter of minutes Kiggings has distracted Juanita and retrieved the handbag. The woman thanks him, laughs, waves at Juanita, and leaves.

As he watches Kiggings expertly handle the cat and get the bag, Terracuso thinks about the coincidence of their association. They are the same age, twenty-six, from the Morris Park section of the Bronx; went to the same school; didn't know each other there; worked here for about ten years; and now have come together to work as a team with the big cats, which both of them love.

Terracuso likes not only Kiggings' competence but his sense of humor, which helps relieve the tedium of their job. They still laugh at the game Kiggings played, using "Puggy," a three-year-old male spotted African hyena. When he was the animal's keeper, Kiggings became weary of visitors' continually asking him, "Is is true hyenas laugh?"

"Sure," Kiggings would say, "tell him a joke and find out."

Some of the visitors would actually walk up to the cage and tell the hyena a joke. When the animal didn't laugh, they would look suspiciously at Kiggings. He would say, "I guess the joke wasn't funny enough." Then he would saunter over to the cage and tell a joke. The hyena always laughed hideously. Unobserved Kiggings had put a piece of raw horsemeat in his pocket.

2:48 P.M.

JOHN BEHLER has just returned to his office in the Administration Building from Kennedy Airport where he went at the request of the United States Customs Bureau. He has been there many times this year. Customs is suspicious of the frequent arrival of poisonous snakes. They think that they may be a "cover" for smuggling drugs. But Customs is also afraid to examine the shipping boxes. Today is the fourth time Behler has found a hidden compartment in the snake container. But, as usual, it was empty. Customs believes that the snake shippers are running tests, that they probably have the containers rigged so that any tampering would be evident. Behler agrees.

His phone rings. "I am Doctor ———," an agitated voice says. "Calling from ———, Connecticut. I have a patient, a young adult, who has a king cobra as a pet. The snake has bitten him. I need cobra antivenin. Do you have any?"

"Yes," Behler says quietly. "But first, let me make it clear that I am not a doctor. When was your patient bitten?"

"Two and a half hours ago!" The doctor is excited.

"Treat the bite as you would any simple puncture wound," Behler calmly instructs the doctor, who splutters with indignation and disbelief. "If your patient had been envenomed, he would have been comatose in six minutes."

Behler, for future reference, gives the doctor the names of several physicians in New York City who are snake-bite experts, and also tells the doctor, who is now calming down, that there are seven thousand snake bites a year in the United States and only about fourteen are fatal.

The zoo has a snake-bite "hotline" it maintains on a twenty-four-hour basis, and it also has a supply of antivenin—both polyvalent, effective for several poisonous species; and .molyvalent, good for single types such as the king cobra—which it shares with doctors who request it. The zoo helps about a dozen people a year bitten by snakes both venomous and harmless.

Most bites are the result of careless handling. An example is that of a man who had caged in his home fourteen puff adders, a gaboon viper, and a Russell's viper, all deadly. A female puff adder had thirteen young, which the man raised, feeding them newborn mice with a four-inch-long pair of forceps. When the young adders were a year old, he was still using the same forceps. The striking range of those adders at that age had extended to nine inches. Consequently, the man was bitten on the hand, and the zoo was called for help.

3 P.M.

THUNDER in the Reptile House; lightning burns; rain falls. In the crocodile display the animals lie, blinking their eyes in the artificial rain, then suddenly slither into their pool.

"What are they doing?" a ten-year-old asks his father.

"Getting out of the rain," the father says; then, realizing the incongruity of what he has said, laughs.

3:10 P.M.

LAST week Papa, a twenty-year-old mandrill, a spectacular baboon from West Africa with a blue and scarlet face and bright-red buttocks, had driven a piece of wood deep

A mandrill, with its spectacular blue-and-scarlet face

into his Achilles' tendon. Dr. Emil Dolensek had managed to remove the piece of wood by first injecting the mandrill with an immobilizing drug while a keeper distracted the big baboon.

As it was a puncture wound prone to infection, the veterinarian later injected the animal with an antibiotic and cleansed the wound three times.

Today was to be the fourth and perhaps last time. Dr. Dolensek enters the Monkey House quietly, while a keeper on the other side of the cage clatters a broomstick against the bars to distract the baboon so the doctor can sneak up and quickly immobilize it with the drug.

This time it doesn't work. As Dolensek climbs a ladder to reach the animal in its high cage, the mandrill whirls. Reaching through the bars with a long, powerful arm, he grabs the veterinarian by the hair and lifts him a foot off the ladder. Still holding on to Dolensek's hair, the baboon slams him forcefully against the cage.

Unable to get enough leverage just with the hair, the mandrill releases it for an instant and shoots the other hand through the cage to grab the veterinarian around the neck. In that split second Dolensek slips off the ladder and escapes.

3:15 P.M.

PETA RADER and Howard Diven are in the outside cage with the young gorillas Mopi and Hodari. The lowland gorilla is an endangered species, and the zoo is extremely interested in raising this pair to maturity. Tunuka, the female in the next cage, had her second offspring, Upweke, a month ago. As child abuse also exists among gorillas, zoo personnel are relieved that mother and child are doing well. A famous case that made national headlines was that of Pattycake, whose parents broke its arm. That baby gorilla was brought here from another zoo until it was nursed to health and could properly fend for itself in the zoo from which it came.

Now, after their daily examination and play session with

Keeper Phil Steindler engages Mopi in conversation.

Peta, the surrogate mother, in a hugging session with Hodari

Knox-Sullivan
Bookmobile

Mopi and Hodari, Peta and Howie move to leave them. The gorillas, not wanting them to go, agilely scamper up the tree in their cage. Knowing they will stay there too long, Peta and Howie call them. But the two won't come down until the keepers start to climb the tree after them. Then they rush down, almost knocking Peta and Howie off the tree.

The crowd of spectators standing before the cage like this. They cheer the young gorillas. As soon as Howie and Peta join Mopi and Hodari on the ground, Mopi reaches into Howie's hip pocket and takes his wallet. The spectators howl with laughter as Howie chases Mopi for five minutes before the little ape will give him the wallet. Everyone thinks it is very funny. Howie does not.

3:20 P.M.

THE Safari Train stops to permit a crowd to walk around it; the driver-lecturer this time is Mike, and his words are audible to the people walking, which causes one man to say to his wife, "Next time, let's take that ride. We'll exercise something besides our feet."

Mike holds his audience. "Giraffes are famous for being the world's tallest animals. These graceful mammals on stilts can reach a height of eighteen feet. Alert, swift, they have excellent eyesight, but when they are lying down or drinking,

The world's tallest animal

they are vulnerable to predation by lions. Man is their only other enemy.

"They live in herds which can consist of as many as seventy animals, although the average herd is about fifteen. Good runners, they can reach a speed of thirty miles per hour. When forced to defend themselves, they kick with their forefeet and give blows with their heads. Although they have long necks, giraffes have only seven neck bones—the same number that a mouse has. That long neck enables giraffes to feed on leaves from acacia trees, which they grasp with their eighteen-inch-long tongues."

3:25 P.M.

AT the World of Birds, Andy Winnegar places the phone on the hook and sighs. He has just received a call from a liquor store on Arthur Avenue, in the Bronx. An excited man tells him that a hummingbird is in the store, zooming around, and he is afraid that someone, bird or customer, is going to be hurt.

Andy gets his special hummingbird net and goes out to the World of Birds' van. He expects that he will be going on several more off-zoo bird hunts this summer. He always does. So adept and gentle with the net that he barely ruffles a feather, he pretends to dislike these outside assignments but actually enjoys them.

3:28 P.M.

As he drives off in the van, Andy remembers another time he went to Arthur Avenue to retrieve a bird. Ten keepers were trying to catch eight African cranes. One of the birds had been purchased from another zoo and was improperly pinioned. It suddenly took off. Even though the wing pinions were ineffective, the bird still couldn't fly too high or too far.

Andy saw it flutter and disappear over what he thought was 185th Street. Rushing there, he had no trouble finding the exotic crane. Behind a board fence, he heard the bird squawking and people shouting.

He looked over the fence. There, in a beautifully tended vegetable garden, with peppers and tomatoes on stakes, were two small boys and an old man chasing the crane. The old man was screaming, "Get that eagle out of here."

3:40 P.M.

REPTILE House. "Junior," the fourteen-foot-long king cobra, loves other snakes. But Junior is a problem. During his first year in the Reptile House he ate eighty snakes— live females of his own species, all introduced as possible mates. At this moment he is being fed one and a half pounds of thawed rattlesnake.

3:45 P.M.

THE second delivery of two thousand live crickets, enough for one week, has just arrived The crickets come from a breeder in Louisiana and, dependent upon size, cost five to six dollars a thousand.

Two keepers are busy opening boxes and quickly placing the live crickets in plastic bags that contain a powdered mixture of calcium and vitamins. The crickets are deficient in calcium. Now, after a second or two in the bags, they emerge chirping. Crickets are a perfect food for the Northeastern Pond Exhibit, which contains lizards, frogs, salamanders, toads, newts, turtles, sunfish, and bluegills.

————————— *4 P.M.* —————————

BEGINNING at the Pony Track when he was ten, Senior Keeper Vincent Nesor, slim, muscular, graying, has been at the zoo for thirty-nine years, longer than any other keeper. He has worked with all of the animals and has a magical way with them. A giant five-foot otter that disliked humans to the point of chasing them followed Nesor around like a pet dog.

Known as "the Whistler," for the obvious reason, Vinnie now is in charge of the buffalo range, the rare-animal range, and the Mongolian wild horses—a testament to his expertness, for the wild horses are the zoo's rarest animals.

Three years ago, when the zoo first acquired the horses—Roxie and Roxanne, the mares; and Bert, the stallion—no one, not even Vinnie, could get near them. But within two weeks he was feeding them peanuts and soon had them coming up and taking them from his pockets. If the stallion nipped him, Vinnie nipped it back. Within three months Vinnie and the three wild horses were friends.

Then the eight-year-old mares were bred for the first time. Bert became protective when the foals were born, but still

: 98   *The only true wild horses—the fierce Mongolians* permitted Vinnie to enter the range and fuss over them. The mares eyed him constantly, but left any action up to the stallion.

The sun is warm today and the Mongolian horses are at the far side of the range, seeking shade. Vinnie is placing a liquid medication in the water trough to protect the young horses from internal parasites.

Bert comes prancing over.

"Hiya, Bert!" Vinnie says.

Bert walks away.

As Vinnie opens the gate, Bert rushes over, glaring, teeth bared.

Before Vinnie can step through, Bert lunges, grabs him by the shoulder blade. Sinking his teeth into the bone, he flips

Vinnie six feet into the air. As Vinnie falls, the stallion bites, then kicks him.

On his knees, Vinnie shouts, fights the horse off long enough to crawl through the gate and close it. Flat on his back, shoulders, nose, arms, hands, knees, cut. Vinnie shouts for help.

Jim Doherty, passing the wild-horse range in his electric cart, hears him. He speeds over, quickly sees Vinnie's condition, the stallion at the gate whinnying and glaring. Doherty gets on the two-way radio and summons help. He kneels, tries to comfort Vinnie until help arrives.

As Vinnie lies dazed, flashing through his mind are visions of the only other time in all these years that he had been hurt by an animal. That time he was keeper of two pandas, Boy and Susie, gifts from China. He raised them from babies until they weighed 400 pounds, pampering them to the point of sleeping with them.

As he hears Doherty asking how he is and faintly answers, "Not bad," Vinnie can still see Boy coming up and throwing his arms around him in an embrace that grew tighter and tighter.

Shouting, fighting, Vinnie finally slipped out of the panda's embrace and left the panda moat. His back felt wet, but there was no pain. Stopping at the small-mammal house, he saw Jack Merritt, who said, "Vinnie, what's the matter? You're all blood!" The panda's long claws had ripped his back badly. Suddenly Vinnie fainted.

Now, hearing the ambulance coming, as he lies outside the wild-horse corral, he again loses consciousness. Rushed to Pelham General Hospital, where he will spend twenty-four hours, and subsequently be away from the zoo for seven weeks, Vinnie is dimly aware of someone sitting beside him in the ambulance.

"Bert didn't mean it," he says clearly. "He was just protecting his herd, the young ones."

4:05 P.M.

EMIL DOLENSEK parks his animal ambulance beside the Lion House and goes inside to see the tigers, as he does at least once every day.

At Dacca's cage, he leans over and carefully puts his nose against hers. The fifteen-year-old Bengal chuffs at the veterinarian as she presses her nose against his and he chuffs back. Dolensek believes that the chuffing is the normal greeting when cats touch noses, the noisy exhaling causing breaths to intermingle so friend can identify friend.

He approaches the cages of Judy and Chica, two Siberians, and gives them his daily nose-to-nose greeting.

Spectators stand and watch in silent awe. The cats and the veterinarian ignore them. Greetings over, Dolensek goes off to check on the hartebeest that broke its horn against the wire fence.

Dr. Dolensek "chuffs" with Dacca.

4:15 P.M.

ON the way, he turns on his two-way radio, something he often forgets. He is being urgently summoned. A unique talipoin monkey has arrived, a pregnant female. It is thought that the monkey had been in labor, but no longer is. It was rushed to the animal hospital, and frantic calls are being sent to Dolensek as he is greeting the tigers.

Zooming the ambulance along the curving paths, Dolensek rushes to his hospital. Examining the monkey, he discovers it has a fetus almost ready to deliver, but has no uterine contractions to force delivery.

He decides that a Caesarean section is necessary immediately. He scrubs, and puts on his operating gown, while an assistant prepares the monkey, strapping it in position on the operating table.

Working with his usual calm intensity, Dolensek, gloved, in cap and mask, makes the abdominal incision, which brings the uterus up into a position where Dolensek then skillfully makes an incision in the fundus. As he completes the sharp, clean incision, a black mummified-looking head appears. Gently, he eases it out. The tiny wet monkey is cleaned and dried, and placed into an incubator. The operation has taken twenty minutes: mother and child, doing well.

4:25 P.M.

A SPECTACULAR ledge of natural rock forms a high, wild skyline. Outlined against it are two Kodiak bears, at 1,600 pounds not only the largest of all bears but also the largest terrestrial carnivores in the world. In a pool beneath the animals on the cliff, two four-year-olds cavort, splashing water, playfully nipping, then hugging each other.

In Frank Casella's brown-bear exhibit there are seven Kodiaks, so called because this particular species comes from Kodiak Island, near the southwestern coast of Alaska.

Keeper Casella uses four words to guide him in caring for his cocoa-colored giants: "smart," "stubborn," "strong," "unpredictable." Not long ago one of the males killed a female bear, without any reason obvious to its keepers.

Now Casella prepares to feed the bears and bed them inside for the night—the procedure for most of the large animals. Locking them up at night while they are being fed enables the keepers to check on appetite, health, and general demeanor at close quarters.

Casella attracts the attention of his charges by the simple medium of calling them. Accustomed to this routine, hungry, all seven bears respond, ambling toward their keeper and their night quarters like great dogs.

As they vanish inside, eight heads pop out from cracks in the cliffside. Then slim, graceful animals jauntily take over what had been bear territory. These are four pairs of red foxes that have been here for two years, raising families, living in harmony with the huge bears through virtue of their agility, secure in their own dens in the rock pile where the bears cannot reach them.

Now, they casually take over ownership of the bear cliff and the pool area, stretching out, basking in the rays of the lowering sun, red coats agleam.

4:30 P.M.

THREE men file silently into the office of the curator of mammals, in the Administration Building, Mark Mac-Namara first, followed by Richard Bergmann and Fred Sterling. Dr. Emil Dolensek is late. He has had an emergency with the birth of a monkey, and a beautiful Thomson's gazelle has been bumping into others in the herd, indicating it has trouble with either balance or vision. Dolensek fears that it is blind, but isn't certain. The men sit quietly until the veterinarian arrives.

After Dolensek is seated, Jim Doherty says, "Let's review Cutie's situation. Emil, would you lead off, please?"

The veterinarian talks about the elephant's failing; she has had chronic kidney disease for a year. Over $3,000 worth of antibiotics have been used on her in less than a year, with discouraging results.

Bergmann points out that she hasn't been eating properly for some time, is losing weight, is very cranky, which finally culminated in the attack on the keeper. He points out that this is most unusual for Cutie, as she is a good-natured, pleasing animal. "She's unhappy," he summarizes.

4:40 P.M.

THE roars are not of rage or even of petulance. Even to visitors, the lion sounds seem lusty, glad-to-be-alive outpourings. Keepers call them "the lucky lions" because they already have their own island, surrounded by a moat that isolates the big cats in their own open area where they live even more successfully than they would in the African wild. Here they have no struggle for existence, no poachers to shoot them for their skins and tails, no animals dealers trapping them for sale. Here they have their own free protected earth.

Mates

Affection

Response

THE sick room at the Reptile House. Pete Brazaitis is examining a five-foot-long animal. Rarely are snakes called anything but animals in the reptile house. This snake has been lethargic, has not been eating, and Pete wants to study it carefully before phoning the veterinarian.

As he replaces it in the cage, the snake rears up and bites him on the arm.

Pete is amazed, then alarmed. He was careless, As he has often preached, that can be fatal. He also is chagrined. This is the first time he has been bitten by a snake. Because there are venomous snakes in the sick room, there is an alarm button. Pete presses it. A loud, gonglike bell activates the anti-venin drill.

A panel electronic indicator in the office flashes the location where the bell was sounded. All keepers respond immediately. Senior Keeper Bob Brandner, Bill Holmstrom, Bruce Foster, and Juan Soto rush to the sick room.

Pete opens the door. He seems nervous. "I have been bitten."

As senior, Brandner takes charge. He is calm, professional. "Is the animal loose?"

"No," Pete says. "Caged."

"Juan, hit the button alerting switchboard in Administra-

tion. Bill, take Pete into another room. Bruce, get the antivenin from the refrigerator."

Brandner himself gets the snakebite fact sheets and stands
by until the antivenin arrives.

He takes the ampul of antivenin, draws off the fluid with
a syringe.

As Brandner moves to inject him, Pete pulls a sponge from
his pocket. "Inject this."

The keepers stare at him. A sponge is used when it is a
practice drill, and a saline solution is used.

"I was nailed by a silly red-tailed rat snake," Pete says.
You guys did pretty good." He looks at his wristwatch. "Four
minutes. Not bad. But next time let's get it down to three."

4:50 P.M.

THE shipment is hours late, but the Brazilian tapir finally
arrives in a crate on a truck, on loan from another zoo. As
two mammal keepers open the crate and attempt to maneuver the 375-pound animal with the long snout and smooth
hide into the tapir enclosure, it makes a sudden bouncing leap
and escapes.

A keeper grabs it, but it is smooth and slippery as a pig;
it slips out of his grasp and runs along a pathway, dodging
two women, who squeal in terror.

The other keeper gets on the two-way radio and alerts the Mammal Department.

There is chagrin, laughter from visitors, considerable frustration, a long chase. It will take thirty keepers forty-five minutes to get the agile animal into the tapir exhibit.

The Brazilian tapir is a "slippery" character.

5 P.M.

VISITORS are leaving the zoo grounds—tired children, exhausted parents.

As they pass the sea-lion pool, the animals bark and undulate like boneless caterpillars, but no one stops. Earlier in the day, when the visitors arrived, it was almost impossible to get the fascinated children away from this first exhibit after entering the main gate.

In front of the Administration Building, Chester Zablocki starts to lower the American flag. Today marks the fourth year he has brought the flag down, ending the visiting hours at the zoo.

5:03 P.M.

FROM the main gate John Siciliano sees that the flag is down, the signal to him that it is time to close Rainey Gates. He waits fifteen minutes while the secretaries and clerical help leave the Administration Building, get into their cars, and drive away. Then he swings the big bronze portals shut. But he waits awhile, in case there are stragglers. He is startled at the sudden, wild, high-pitched whoops of the white-handed gibbons on Gibbon Island, not far from the main gate. In twelve years he has not become inured to that maniacal sound that seems just feet away.

5:30 P.M.

SICILIANO locks the gates. His zoo day has ended.

For many others it has not. Their day in the life of their zoo is timed by a clock without hands.

5:55 P.M.

JOE SPADAFINO is making a slow tour of the zoo grounds on his cycle.

Suddenly, from one of the winding paths, a man darts out in front of him. Spadafino brakes.

The man has a desperate look. "I lost the keys to my ignition. We're stranded! We're way over at the Crotona entrance and I can't find anybody!"

Spadafino walks his cycle beside the man, calming him, until they reach his car. A woman and three children are huddled, frightened, inside.

"Thank God!" the woman says. "I thought we'd be here all night." One child is crying.

Spadafino expertly "jumps" their ignition, gets the car started, then guides them over to the service entrance and lets them out.

<hr>

7:15 P.M.

IT is that serene moment of a summer evening when dusk hangs like smoke, and night begins to gather in high purple patches. Shadows are seeking corners and the electric lights seem dim and ineffectual in the office of the director, where Dr. F. Wayne King, James Doherty, and Dr. Emil Dolensek sit facing William Conway.

Conway will have to make a difficult decision, but he leans heavily upon his staff, which he believes to be the best in zoodom. In his usual, straightforward manner, he asks Dolensek, then Doherty, to review all aspects of Cutie's illness.

The mood is somber; Cutie is a favorite of every man in the room. The elephant has been here long before most of them, and is one of the foundation animals upon which the zoo has built its reputation.

Finally, after Dolensek and Doherty have finished, Conway, slowly, reluctantly, says, "If Cutie is in constant pain, and has absolutely no chance of recovery, just additional pain and discomfort, I don't see that we have any other alternative but euthanasia. Do any of you, gentlemen?"

The men shake their heads.

Emil Dolensek feels a sudden small panic start deep in his stomach. Although his demeanor is calm, professional, he is the first to leave.

——— 7:30 P.M. ———

CHILDREN'S ZOO. A rooster crows nervously; Kanga, the Norwegian fjord pony, whinnies, a sound like that of wind trapped in a tunnel. Susan Basford, operations supervisor, and Jill Murphy, mistress of the riding track, are still here. Susan is preparing to take the two young wild boars home with her. They must be fed every two hours, and Susan feels the best way to do this is to keep them with her.

Jill Murphy has her own problem. The axis-deer fawn the Children's Zoo is raising needs the body warmth at night that its mother has refused it. The wobbly little spotted deer can barely walk but already follows Jill around as if she were its mother. Jill will take it home and sleep on the floor with it all night.

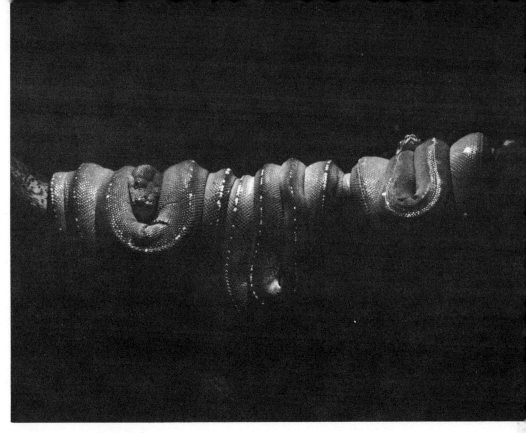

Green pythons at rest

7:55 P.M.

THE telephone rings in the zoo residence of Dr. King. A keeper at the Reptile House is disturbed. A twelve-foot reticulated python has been lacerated, is bleeding, needs expert attention, and the keeper can't locate the veterinarian, who doesn't have an apartment at the zoo. One of the several hats Dr. King wears is that of herpetologist. His apartment phone is also the zoo's "reptile hotline."

"Keep the snake's wounds moist with sterile saline solution," he advises. "I'll call Dr. Dolensek at home, and come right over and have a look."

8 P.M.

WORLD of Darkness. There is action everywhere in the ghostly blue moonlight: bats and screech owls in flight, their wings making a soft hiss; a nine-banded armadillo waddles; in a tree a prehensile-tailed porcupine rattles quills.

Cosmo Barbetto is on the lower floor, where there are no exhibits but where five big boa constrictors are fed. Each snake is placed in a large plastic barrel with three rats—its weekly ration; the cover of the barrel is replaced and the boas eat in privacy. Cosmo uses this system to ascertain that they are eating properly.

Today, one of the keepers didn't replace one cover correctly and a boa escaped. Because the door to this section is used often, is opened and closed at all hours, the enormous snake could be anyplace in the World of Darkness.

Cosmo has spent two hours searching. Using a flashlight, even though he has the electric lights on, he carefully checks every inch of the room. He is about to give it up when the beam of his light strikes a slightly speckled surface on an overhead drain pipe.

Quickly, Cosmo gets a ladder from the next room. Placing it under the discolored pipe, he climbs and finds the boa stretched full out, sound asleep. Such is the marvel of the natural camouflage of its skin; it could have lain there for days, sleeping off its rat binge, without being observed.

Cosmo carefully lifts the heavy snake, adjusts it on his shoulder, descends the ladder, and places the boa in its cage.

9:30 P.M.

MARK MacNAMARA has had a strenuous day, and will have a restless night.

He has brought to his zoo apartment a baby brush-tailed phalanger, a marsupial native to Australia. This animal's mother died when it was four weeks old and still in her pouch. Usually phalangers remain in the pouch for six months, nursing all of the time, emerging fully developed.

Mark faces a challenge with this partially developed animal. He has it in an incubator and for three days must feed it twelve times a day, then every four hours for two weeks. If he is successful, this will be the first time that a phalanger will have been hand-raised from this age.

Wearily now, a baby's bottle of warm milk in his hand, he

approaches the little creature looking at him with black, round, staring eyes.

He will have the phalanger in his apartment for five months.

10 P.M.

IN the Reptile House, John Behler and Pete Brazaitis prepare for a trip to Kennedy Airport. Both are tired, but exhilarated.

In two hours a special creature will arrive from the Munich Zoo: a male Chinese alligator, a rare and endangered species found only in the Yangtze River Valley of China. The

Night descends on the Bronx Zoo.

alligators haven't been exported from China for twenty years. There are only four in the United States, and Behler and Brazaitis will entrust the task of picking it up and delivering it to the zoo to no one else.

They know it is a large reptile, well over six feet long, and that it will be difficult to transfer and transport. But months ago Brazaitis solved the crocodile-and-alligator-transport problem with a sudden, almost macabre brainstorm: What about a coffin liner? He called a local casket company and discovered they made large coffin liners sturdily constructed of fitted pine. Already Brazaitis has successfully shipped several alligators to other zoos in them.

Midnight

MAMMAL Curator James Doherty has been unable to sleep. The decision to exercise euthanasia on Cutie has disturbed him deeply. She has become a symbol of the Bronx Zoo itself. Doherty takes a flashlight, leaves his apartment, and walks under a sky aburst with stars to the Elephant House, grateful that he is not Emil Dolensek, who will have to perform the sad task shortly after the sun rises.

As he opens the door to the Elephant House, the pungent odor of dung intermingles with that of fresh hay in a curiously wild aroma that makes him think of far-off jungles and a wild world of freedom, and he wonders if Cutie has had a happy life here at the zoo. He doesn't bother to switch on the lights, he knows Cutie's stall almost as well as he knows his own bedroom. He hopes she is sleeping peacefully during her last night on earth.

The beam of his flashlight probes the darkness of the elephant stall like a persistent finger until it finds the big animal at the far end, flat on the floor.

She is sleeping. Doherty heaves a sigh of relief. Cutie hasn't been able to sleep in days.

But as he keeps the light on her, the experienced mammal expert detects that there is absolutely no motion; the big gray shape is as still as death.

Doherty blinks back tears, turns off the flashlight, and leaves the Elephant House.

Emil Dolensek will not have to perform that dreaded duty after all.

BOOKS BY JACK DENTON SCOTT

Novels

TOO LIVELY TO LIVE (with Anne Damer)
ELEPHANT GRASS
SPARGO

Travel

FORESTS OF THE NIGHT
PASSPORT TO ADVENTURE
JOURNEY INTO SILENCE

Natural History
Photoessays with photographer Ozzie Sweet:

THE LOGGERHEAD TURTLE
THAT WONDERFUL PELICAN
CANADA GEESE
RETURN OF THE BUFFALO
LITTLE DOGS OF THE PRAIRIE
THE GULLS OF SMUTTYNOSE ISLAND
DISCOVERING THE AMERICAN STORK

Essays

SPEAKING WILDLY
THE SURVIVORS

Juveniles

PUG INVADES THE FIFTH COLUMN (with Donald Cook)
THE DULUTH MONGOOSE

Cookbooks

THE COMPLETE BOOK OF PASTA
FEAST OF FRANCE (with Antoine Gilly)
INFORMAL DINNERS FOR EASY ENTERTAINING
(with Maria Luisa Scott)
COOK LIKE A PEASANT, EAT LIKE A KING (with Maria Luisa Scott)
MASTERING MICROWAVE COOKING (with Maria Luisa Scott)
THE WORLD OF PASTA (with Maria Luisa Scott)
THE BEST OF THE PACIFIC COOKBOOK